Dear Parent:

Your child's love of reading starts here!

Every child learns to read in a different way and at his or her own speed. Some go back and forth between reading levels and read favorite books again and again. Others read through each level in order. You can help your young reader improve and become more confident by encouraging his or her own interests and abilities. From books your child reads with you to the first books he or she reads alone, there are I Can Read Books for every stage of reading:

SHARED READING
Basic language, word repetition, and whimsical illustrations, ideal for sharing with your emergent reader

BEGINNING READING
Short sentences, familiar words, and simple concepts for children eager to read on their own

READING WITH HELP
Engaging stories, longer sentences, and language play for developing readers

READING ALONE
Complex plots, challenging vocabulary, and high-interest topics for the independent reader

I Can Read Books have introduced children to the joy of reading since 1957. Featuring award-winning authors and illustrators and a fabulous cast of beloved characters, I Can Read Books set the standard for beginning readers.

A lifetime of discovery begins with the magical words **"I Can Read!"**

Visit www.icanread.com for information on enriching your child's reading experience.

Visit www.zonderkidz.com/icanread for more faith-based I Can Read! titles from Zonderkidz.

He made all kinds of creatures
that move along the ground.
And God saw that it was good.
—*Genesis 1:24-26*

ZONDERKIDZ

Spiders, Snakes, Bees, and Bats
Copyright © 2010 by Zonderkidz

An **I Can Read Book**

Requests for information should be addressed to:

Zonderkidz, 3900 *Sparks Drive SE, Grand Rapids, Michigan 49546*

Library of Congress Cataloging-in-Publication Data
    Spiders, snakes, bees, and bats.
       p. cm. — (I can read!)
         ISBN 978-0-310-72007-2 (softcover)
    1. Spiders—Juvenile literature. 2. Vertebrates—Juvenile literature. I. Zonderkidz.
    QL458.4.S647 2010
    590—dc22   2009041261

All Scripture quotations, unless otherwise indicated, are taken from The Holy Bible, *New International Version®, NIV®.* Copyright © 1973, 1978, 1984, 2011 by Biblica, Inc.® Used by permission of Zondervan. All rights reserved worldwide. www.Zondervan.com. The "NIV" and "New International Version" are trademarks registered in the United States Patent and Trademark Office by Biblica, Inc.®

Any internet addresses (websites, blogs, etc.) and telephone numbers in this book are offered as a resource. They are not intended in any way to be or imply an endorsement by Zondervan, nor does Zondervan vouch for the content of these sites and numbers for the life of this book.

No part of this publication may be reproduced, stored in a retrieval system, or transmitted in any form or by any means — electronic, mechanical, photocopy, recording, or any other — except for brief quotations in printed reviews, without the prior permission of the publisher.

Zonderkidz is a trademark of Zondervan.

I Can Read® and I Can Read Book® are trademarks of HarperCollins Publishers.

Editor: Mary Hassinger
Art direction & design: Sarah Molegraaf

Printed in China

19 20 21 22 23 24 /DSC/ 12 11 10 9 8 7

···MADE·BY·GOD···

Spiders, Snakes, Bees, and Bats

Contents

Spiders 5

Snakes 12

Bees 19

Bats 26

God made everything.

It is all good.

He made the gentle butterfly and

the hairiest, biggest…

SPIDER!

Spiders are not really insects.

They are animals called arachnids.

Spiders are found almost everywhere.

God made about 30,000 kinds of spiders.

Most have eight legs and eight eyes.

Spiders are carnivorous.

They eat only meat.

Spiders might be pests,
but they eat many bugs that bug us,
like mosquitoes.
To help catch food, most spiders use webs.

Spider body parts called spinnerets make silk to build webs. Webs are used as homes, to catch food, and for cocoons.

There are many kinds of webs — spiral orb and funnel are two.

A well-known spider is the tarantula.
Tarantulas are furry.
They can grow to be nine or ten inches—like a dinner plate!
Some people have pet tarantulas.

God made everything.

It is all good.

He made the cutest puppy

and the longest, creepiest…

SNAKE!

Snakes are reptiles.

They are found almost everywhere.

Snakes live in deserts, lakes, forests, and fields.

Snakes are covered with smooth,
dry scales that protect them.
Snakes shed their old scales.
If they do not fall off,
the snake might get sick.

Some snakes are hatched from eggs.
Others come out of their mother.
No matter how they are born,
all snakes have special bones that
twist, bend, and curl.

Snakes smell with their tongues.

The tongue collects smells.

It goes back into the snake's mouth

to a spot called Jacobson's Organ.

It tells the snake whose scent

is on the tongue.

One very tiny snake is called a thread snake. It eats ant and termite eggs. The longest snakes are pythons and anacondas. They eat eggs, fish, frogs, and small rodents. If they eat a big meal, these snakes eat only four or five times a year!

God made everything.

It is all good.

He made the prettiest rose

and the buzzing, stinging…

BEE!

Bees are insects.
They have six legs, five eyes, four wings, a nectar pouch, and stomach.
Bees are found in many places but do not like cold weather.
In winter, bees stay in their hive to keep warm.
They eat the honey they made all summer.

God made more than 10,000 kinds of bees.

Bees live in hives or nests.

A small hive may have 20,000 bees!

There is only one queen, and she is in charge for two to three years.

The queen bee can lay
2,000 eggs every day.
She has lots of help in the hive.
Female worker bees do all the work.
There are hundreds of male bees
called drones.
The drones have no stingers.
Their main job is to help the queen
make babies.

Bees have two jobs.
Bees make honey from
pollen and nectar in flowers.
One bee visits 4,000 flowers
to make one tablespoon of honey!
When looking for pollen,
a bee can fly six miles and
travel fifteen miles an hour!

Bees have a job called pollination.
Their sticky legs help pollen
get from one plant to another.
Without the help of bees,
many plants may not grow.

God made everything.

It is all good.

He made the big, strong eagle

and the squeaky, scary-looking…

BAT!

Bats are the only flying mammal in the world.
They use their wings for flying and holding things like food.

God made over 1,000 kinds of bats.

They live all over the world.

Bats sleep in roosts.

Roosts are found in places

like caves and hollow trees.

Bats sleep upside-down.

This makes it easier for them to

take off fast, if necessary.

Bats help people by eating
pesky bugs like mosquitoes.
A single brown bat can eat 1,200
mosquitoes in one hour!
Other bats eat fruit, fish, and frogs.
Bats mostly eat at night.
They use sounds that people cannot
hear to help find food in the dark.
This is called echo-location.

Bat babies are called pups.
When bats grow up, they like to live and fly in large groups called colonies.

One of the largest colonies of bats
is in the state of Texas.
About twenty million bats
live together in one cave and share
a dinner of about 200 tons of bugs…
each night!